D1171805

Keys and Symbols on Maps

Meg Greve

ROURKE PUBLISHING

Vero Beach, Florida 32964

www.rourkepublishing.com

PHOTO CREDITS: © Alexandr Dvorak: Title Page; © Mike Clarke: 3; © exi5: 4, 6, 14, 18, 20; © iofoto: 5, 21; © DIGIcal: 7; © Günay Mutlu: 8, 12; © jan kranendonk: 9, 23; © Windzepher: 11, 22; © Aimin Tang: 13, 22; © Gene Chutka: 15; © joannawnuk: 17; © Fernando Delvalle: 19;

Edited by Jeanne Sturm

Cover design by Nicola Stratford bdpublishing.com
Interior design by Tara Raymo

Library of Congress Cataloging-in-Publication Data

Greve, Meg.
  Keys and symbols on maps / Meg Greve.
      p. cm. -- (Little world geography)
  Includes bibliographical references and index.
  ISBN 978-1-60694-419-6 (hard cover)
  ISBN 978-1-60694-535-3 (soft cover)
  ISBN 978-1-60694-586-5 (bilingual)
  1. Map reading--Juvenile literature. 2. Maps--Symbols--Juvenile literature.
I. Title.
  GA130.G748 2010
  912.01'48--dc22
                            2009006021

Rourke Publishing
Printed in the United States of America, North Mankato, Minnesota
062310
062210LP-B

www.rourkepublishing.com - rourke@rourkepublishing.com
Post Office Box 643328 Vero Beach, Florida 32964

2

Look at a **map.**
What do you see?

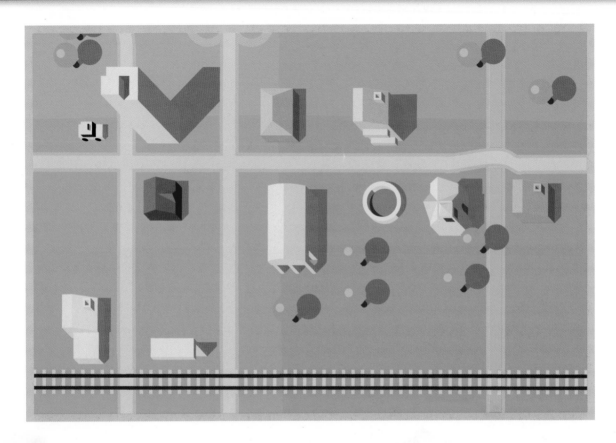

You see **symbols** and a **key.**

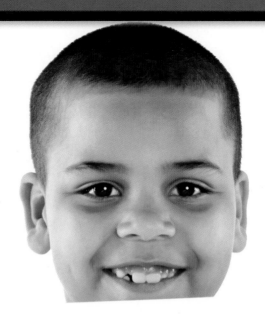

KEY

Street

River

 Railroad Tracks

Parking Lot

Houses

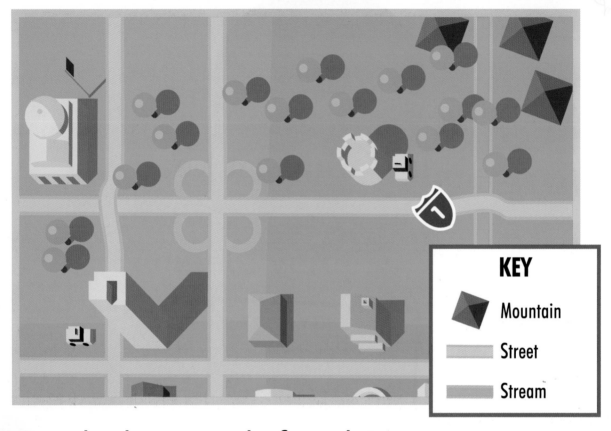

KEY

⬙ Mountain

▬ Street

▬ Stream

Symbols stand for bigger things, like **mountains**, streets, or even streams.

KEY
- • City
- —— Street
- —— River
- ✈ Airport

Symbols are so very small.

Maps and **globes** can't show it all.

KEY
- • City
- — Street
- — River
- ✈ Airport

A **city** might be a little dot.

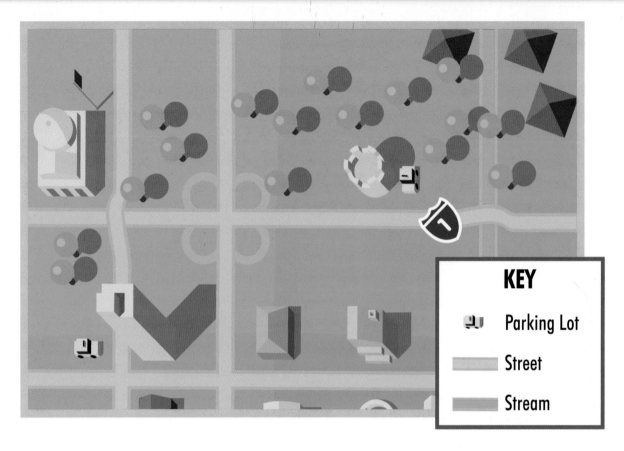

KEY

Parking Lot

Street

Stream

A car might mean a parking lot.

PURIFIED WAT

Look in the corner to find the key, a handy tool to explain what you see.

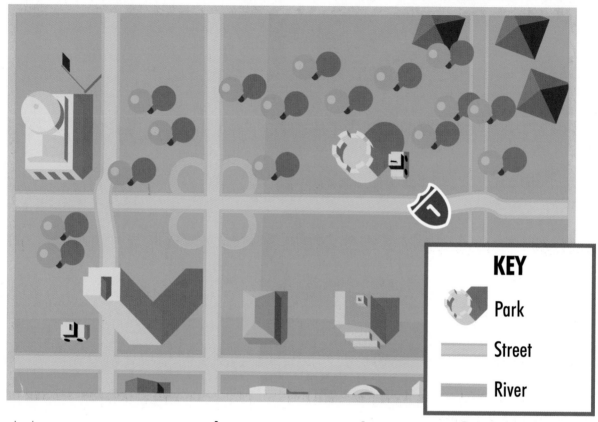

KEY

Park

Street

River

Maps can show us lots of things, like giant rivers or parks with swings.

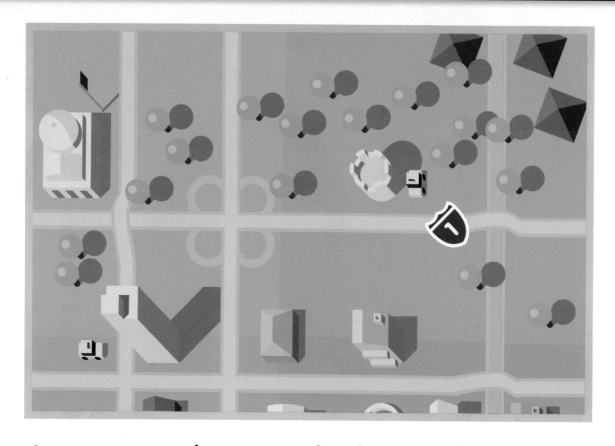

Just use the symbols and
the key, reading maps is fun
and easy!

GLOSSARY

 **city** (SIT-ee): A city is a very large town with lots of people living in it. Cities have lots of streets, buildings, and stores.

 **globes** (GLOHBS): Globes are round spheres that show the entire Earth. Globes contain symbols and colors that stand for bigger things.

 **key** (KEE): A key shows what the symbols stand for on a map. You can usually find the key in one of the bottom corners on a map. Sometimes a key is called a legend.

map (MAP): A map is a flat drawing of an area. There are maps of streets, towns, cities, the world, and much more. Maps contain symbols and colors, which all stand for something larger.

mountains (MOUN-tuhns): Mountains are parts of the land that are very high. Some mountains were created by glaciers or volcanoes.

symbols (SIM-buhls): Symbols are little pictures on a map that stand for bigger things. An airplane symbol stands for an airport, and blue lines show rivers.

Index

Websites to Visit

www.maps4kids.com

www.fedstats.gov/kids/mapstats/

http://kids.nationalgeographic.com/

About the Author

Meg Greve lives in Chicago with her husband, daughter, and son. She loves to study maps and imagines traveling to new and different places.

24